LEVEL THREE
piano repertoire

By David Carr Glover
and Louise Garrow

David Carr Glover
PIANO LIBRARY

Piano Repertoire - Level III
Melodies from Famous Composers
by
David Carr Glover
and
Louise Garrow

Foreword

The materials in this book are arrangements of melodies from the masters, which will in turn lead to the original keyboard music of Bach, Mozart, Beethoven, and Schumann in Piano Repertoire - Level IV.

The transition from arranged materials to original master works is an important stage in the musical development of the student. Often the original works are assigned before the student is technically equipped to play them. The authors feel that the arrangements in this book will stimulate the continued interest in piano study and help create a love and appreciation of good music.

If, upon completion of this book, the student is not yet mature enough for original master works, it is best to find additional music within his limitations. Let us not discourage our students by giving them music for which they are not ready. A wealth of material is available for every grade level. The important thing is that the student be exposed to a wide variety of such material, for in this way we are giving him a solid background in technic and style.

Materials Correlated with "The Piano Student" — Level III

© 1967 FIRST DIVISION PUBLISHING CORPORATION
© Assigned 1968 BELWIN-MILLS PUBLISHING CORP. (ASCAP)
All Rights Assigned to and Controlled by ALFRED MUSIC PUBLISHING CO., INC.
All Rights Reserved.   Printed in USA.

Contents

Trio
from "Symphony in E♭"

MOZART
arr. GARROW

Norwegian Dance

GRIEG
arr. GLOVER

F.D.L.326

Menuetto

from Symphony #1

BEETHOVEN
arr. GLOVER

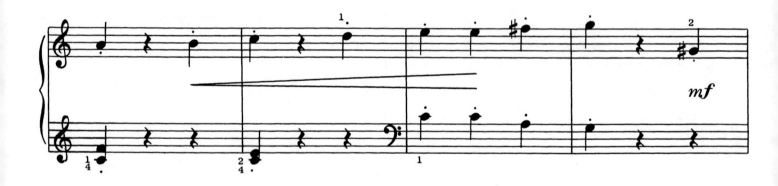

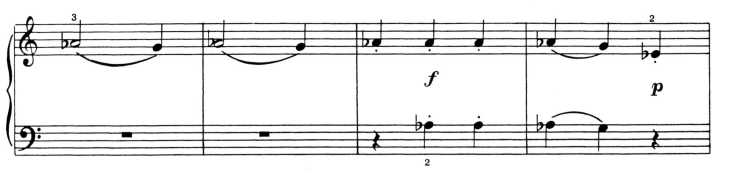

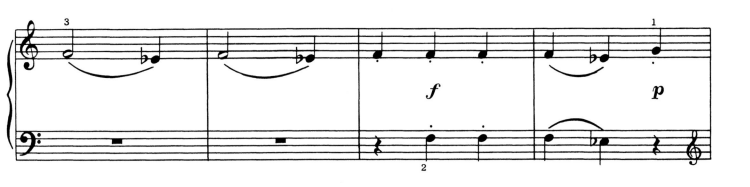

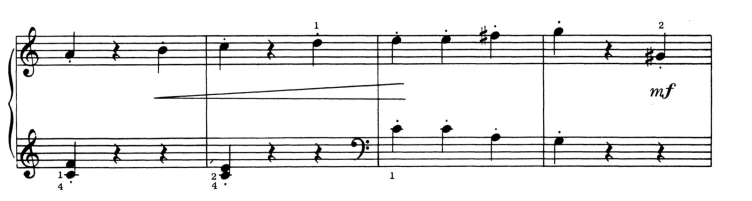

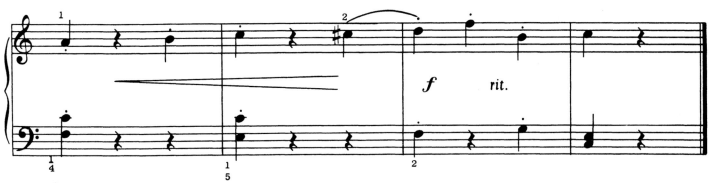

Elegie
Op 10

MASSENET
arr. GLOVER

Slowly with much feeling

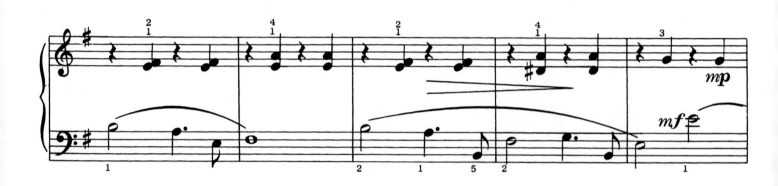

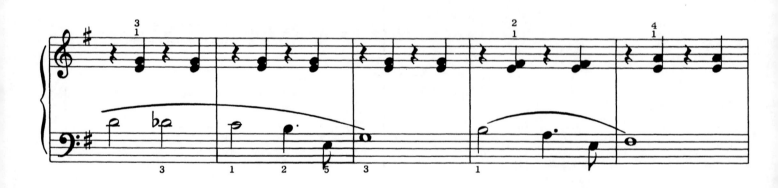

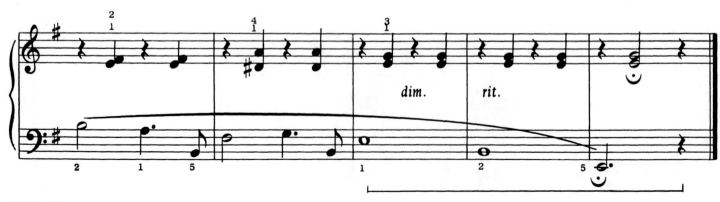

Finale

from Symphony #1

BRAHMS
arr. GLOVER

Moderately fast

Melody
from "Oberon"

WEBER
arr. GARROW

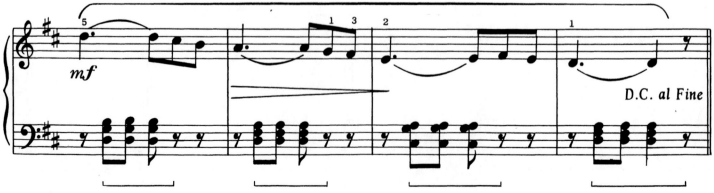

Bacchanale

from Samson and Delilah

SAINT-SAËNS
arr. GLOVER

Funeral March
from Sonata #2-Bb Minor

CHOPIN
arr. GARROW

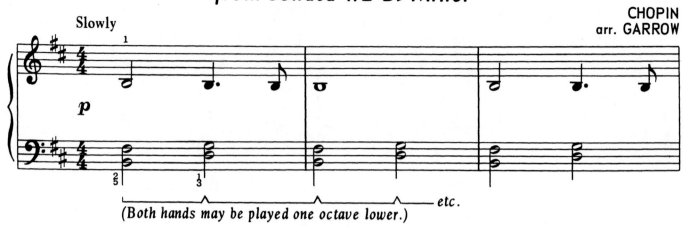

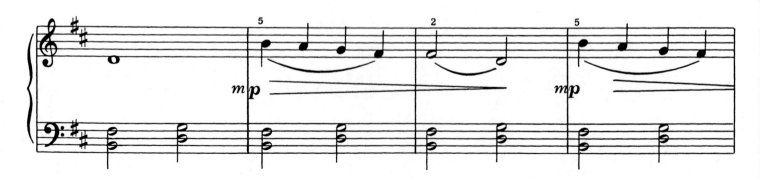

F.D.L.326

War March of the Priests

from Athalia

MENDELSSOHN
arr. GLOVER

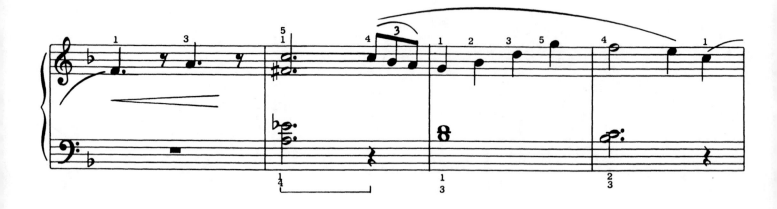

Bouree

from The Second Suite for Solo Violin

BACH
arr. GLOVER

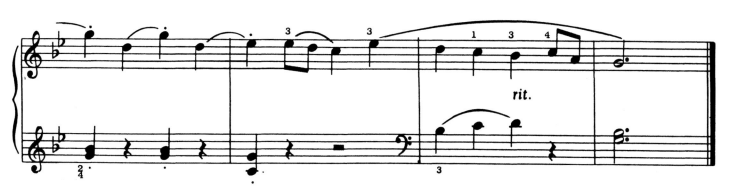

F.D.L.326

Danse Macabre

SAINT-SAËNS
arr. GARROW

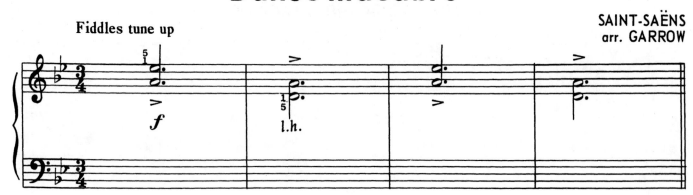

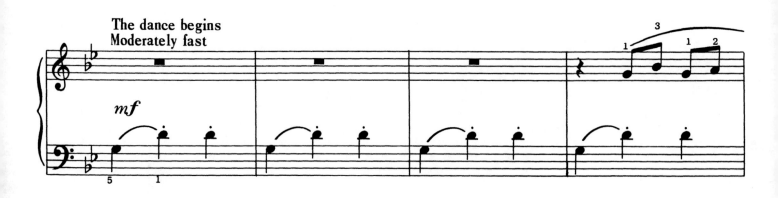

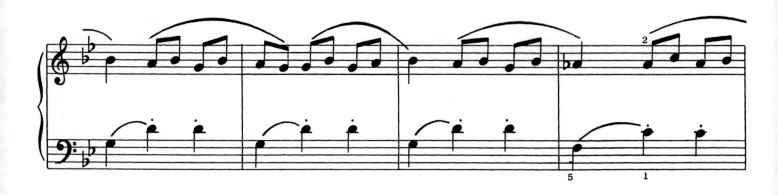

F.D.L.326

Trumpet March
from Aïda

VERDI
arr. GLOVER

March tempo

Theme

from 2nd Movement, Piano Concerto B♭ Minor

TSCHAIKOWSKY
arr. GLOVER

F.D.L.326

Theme
from "Fifth Symphony"

BEETHOVEN
arr. GLOVER - GARROW

Allegro con brio

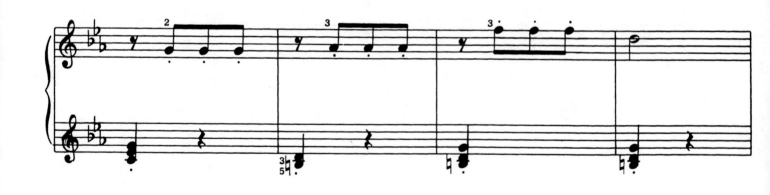

F.D.L.326

Scheherazade

RIMSKY - KORSAKOV
arr. GLOVER

Slowly with much expression

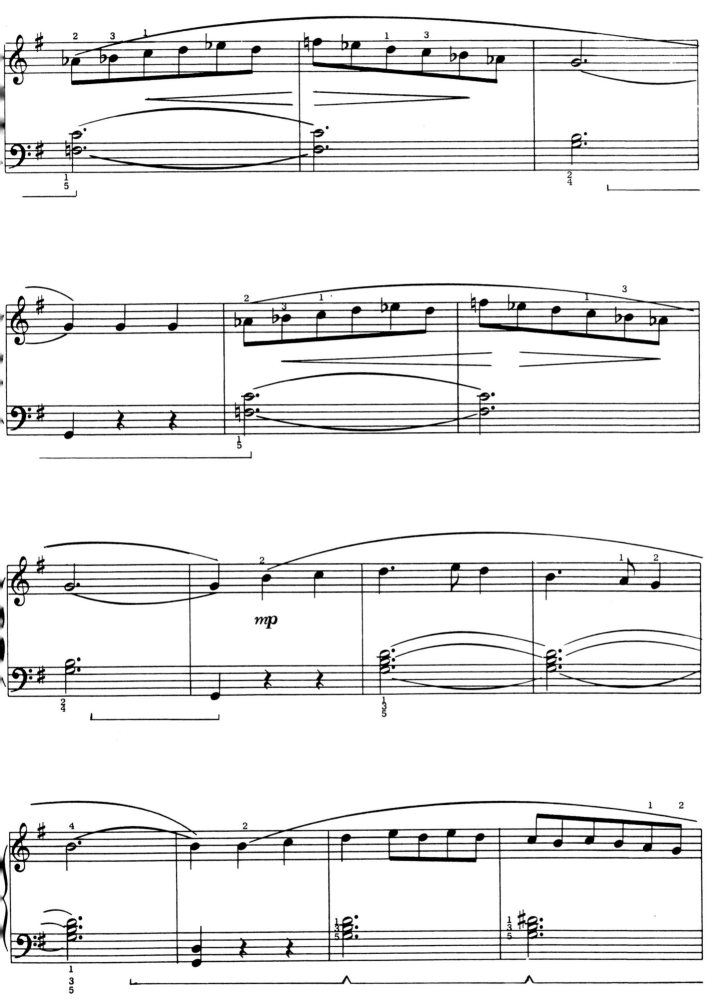

F.D.L.326

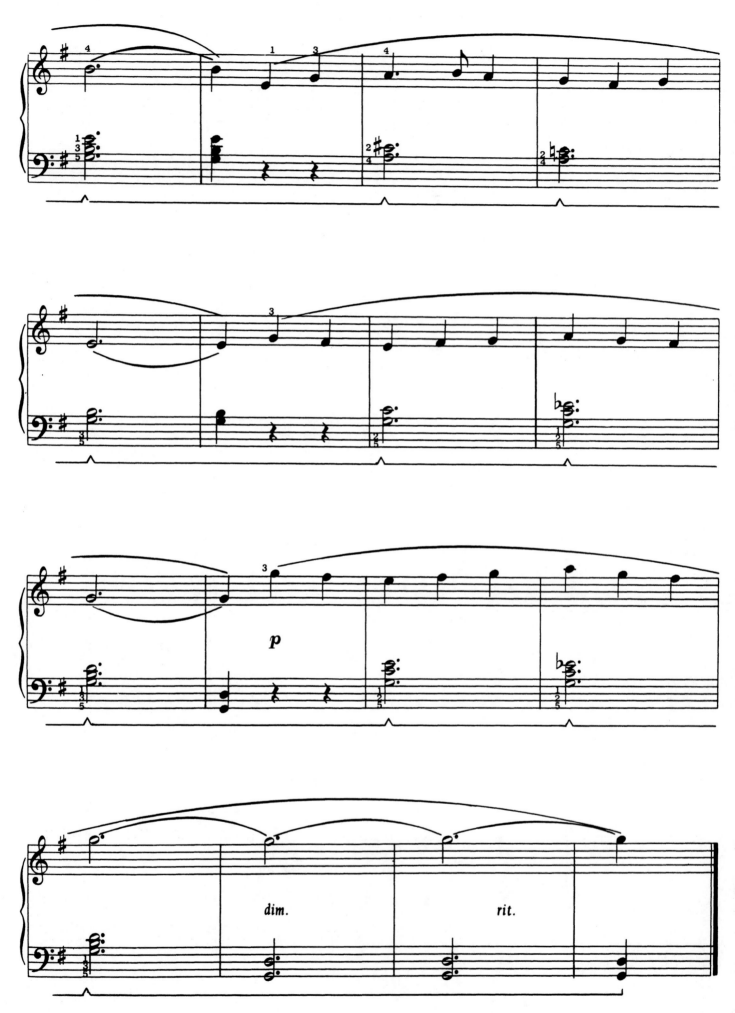

Melody in F

RUBINSTEIN
arr. GLOVER

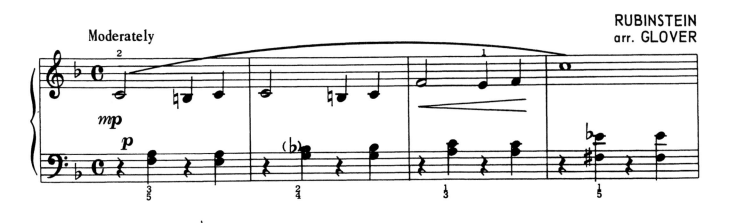

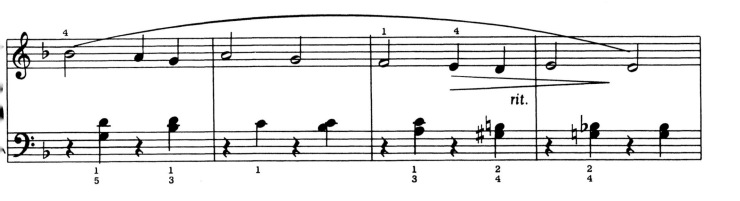

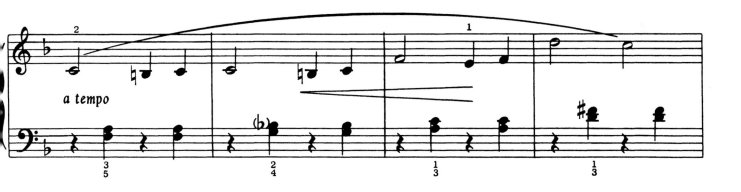

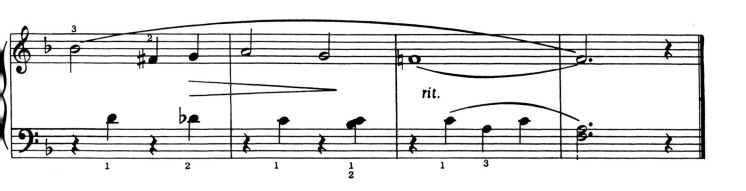

F.D.L.326

Bridal Chorus
from Lohengrin

RICHARD WAGNER
arr. GARROW

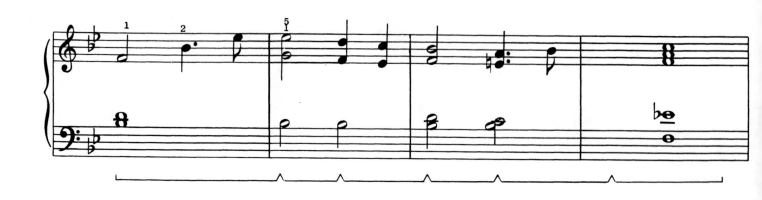

Etude

FREDRIC CHOPIN
arr. GLOVER

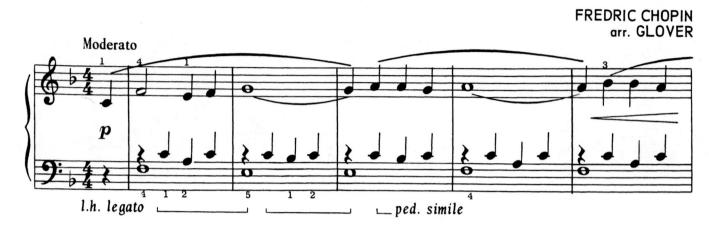

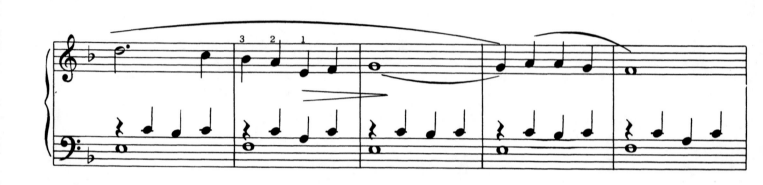

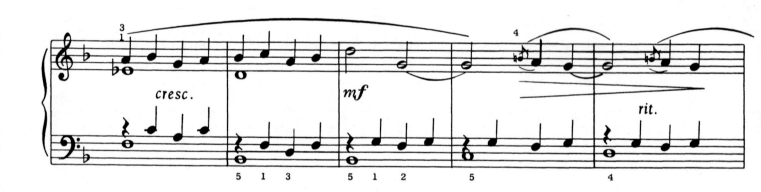

F.D.L. 326

Valse Noble

FRANZ SCHUBERT
arr. GLOVER

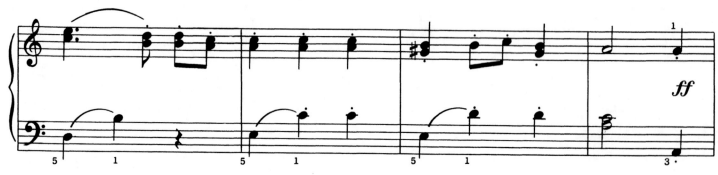

F.D.L. 326

Ballet Music
from"Rosamunde"

FRANZ SCHUBERT
arr. GLOVER

.D.L.326

Funeral March of A Marionette

CHARLES GOUNOD
arr. GLOVER

Moderato